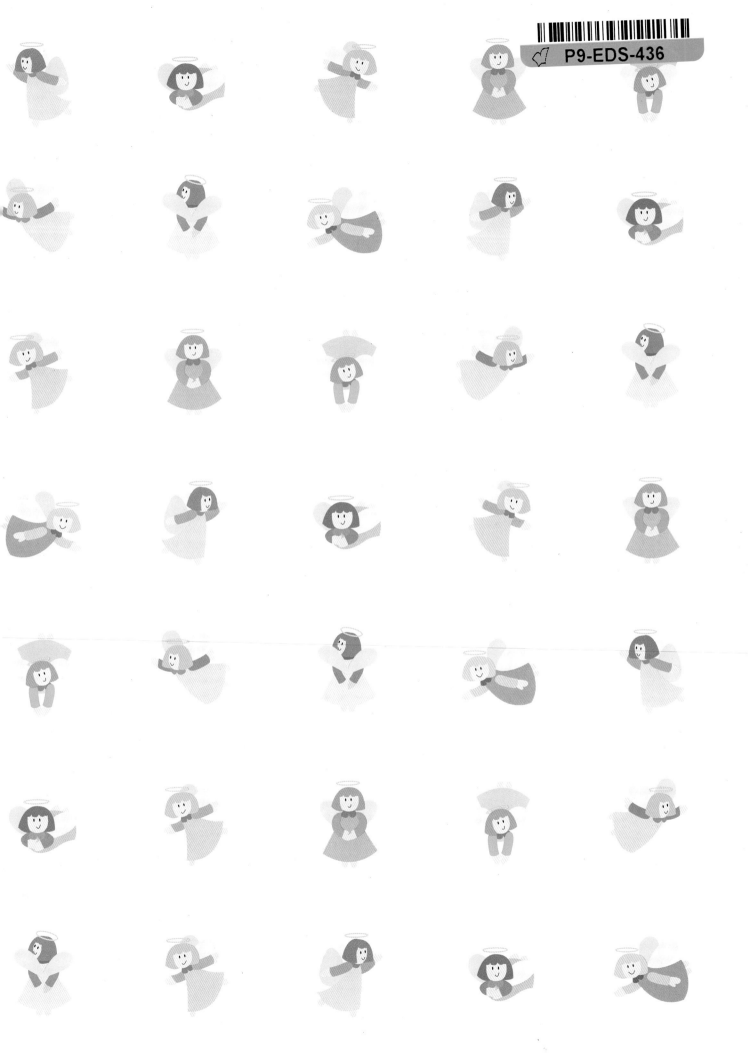

Cross Stitch
ANGELS

Over 30 inspirational new designs

David & Charles

A DAVID & CHARLES BOOK

First published in the UK in 2004
Designs Copyright © Sue Cook, Claire Crompton, Maria Diaz,
Joan Elliott, Helen Philipps and Lesley Teare 2004
Text, photography and layout Copyright © David & Charles 2004

Distributed in North America
by F&W Publications, Inc.
4700 East Galbraith Road
Cincinnati, OH 45236
1-800-289-0963

Sue Cook, Claire Crompton, Maria Diaz, Joan Elliott,
Helen Philipps and Lesley Teare have asserted their right to be
identified as authors of this work in accordance with the
Copyright, Designs and Patents Act, 1988.

A catalogue record for this book is available
from the British Library.
ISBN 0 7153 1648 6

Executive Commissioning Editor Cheryl Brown
Desk Editor Ame Verso
Executive Art Editor Ali Myer
Art Editor Prudence Rogers
Project Editor and chart preparation Lin Clements
Photography Kim Sayer and Lucy Mason

Printed in Italy by STIGE
for David & Charles
Brunel House   Newton Abbot   Devon

Visit our website at www.davidandcharles.co.uk

David & Charles books are available from all good bookshops;
alternatively you can contact our Orderline on (0)1626 334555 or
write to us at FREEPOST EX2110, David & Charles Direct, Newton
Abbot TQ12 4ZZ (no stamp required UK mainland).

Contents

Introduction

This cross stitch collection by six top designers has been inspired by angels;
by all the memorable qualities of angels – the love, friendship,
guidance and hope they bring – and by the distinctive images
of angels that have evolved over the centuries.

Many people all over the world believe in guiding spirit beings, or angels, who act as God's messenger. In fact, the English word 'angel' is derived from the Greek *ággelos*, which means messenger. The idea of angels probably evolved originally from the winged deities described in Sumerian, Egyptian and Semitic beliefs. Tribal cultures and ancient civilizations believed that spiritual beings would guide and protect them and messages from such beings were looked for in dreams, signs and intuitions.

Christian ideas about angels were further developed from the 11th to 12th centuries, particularly through the teachings of Saint Thomas Aquinas who believed that angels filled the gap between God and humans. Ideas about angels were also influenced by John Milton's *Paradise Lost*, an epic English poem describing the fall of Satan and other Biblical stories.

Judaism, Christianity and Islam all have a rich tradition of belief in divinities or angels. For the Christian religion, models for angels were found in pagan worship of such gods as Hermes, Eros and Iris, and these figures were eventually transmuted into images of winged, androgenous humans decorating the churches of Europe from the Middle Ages onwards.

Angels are commonly portrayed as all sweetness and light but some stereotyping and sentimentalization has taken place over the centuries. Many of the descriptions of angels in the Bible show them as made of far meatier stuff – fierce guardians of heaven and ruthless judges – meant for mankind's growth not his comfort.

Nowadays we prefer to focus on all of the positive aspects of angels and this is what this book is all about – a celebration in cross stitch of the uplifting, life-affirming qualities of angels. The six designers featured have provided a truly wonderful selection of angel designs, ranging from medieval-style images to those inspired by folk art, from dreamy romance to cute, impish scenes.

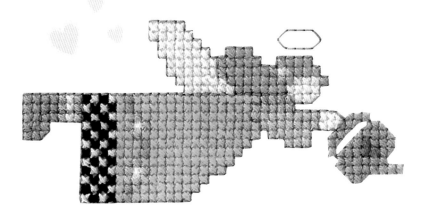

Joan Elliott's Angels of the World is a lovely wall hanging embellished with beads and metallic threads. Her second design, Be An Angel, has sweet cherubs encouraging every family member to heed the 'house rules'.

Claire Crompton has designed twelve gorgeous angel birthday cards, featuring the birthstone for each month.

Sue Cook's enchanting angel birth sampler with its soft colours and nursery-style images is perfect to welcome a new arrival. There is also a card and door hanger that are quick to stitch.

Lesley Teare's romantic Wedding Angel sampler is simply dreamy, a perfect memento of a special occasion. She has also created a delightful angel alphabet in a Victorian style which you are sure to stitch again and again.

Helen Philipps' six hobby angel designs are wonderfully fresh and sure to please friends and family alike. Their charming folk-art style is perfect for today's country-style and Shaker-inspired interiors.

Maria Diaz's three golden angels have a Renaissance quality. They are presented in a collage style with a variety of borders, making the designs very versatile. Her collection of little blue angels is equally adaptable, filled with fun-loving, pixie-like cherubs.

Each chapter contains all you need to stitch the designs and make up the projects, with full step-by-step instructions and easy-to-follow colour charts. There are also many suggestions throughout describing other ways to use the designs. At the end of the book is a short section on the equipment you will need, the basic techniques and the stitches required. The designs are shown worked in DMC stranded cotton (floss) but for those of you who prefer Anchor threads there is a conversion table on page 102. There is also a good list of suppliers to help you track down the exact materials used in the projects.

Angels are a wonderfully inspiring subject. Not only are the many glorious images of angels perfect for interpretation in cross stitch, but in stitching these designs you can be sure of sending the love, friendship and hope that angels symbolize to all your family and friends. There's an angel here for everyone.

Angels of the World

'We should not forget to entertain strangers lest we entertain angels unawares.' The words from the Bible (Hebrews, chapter 13, verse 14) featured in this beautiful design are particularly relevant in the global civilization we now live in.

This picture is also a reminder that the belief in angels is not only an enduring one throughout human history but one that spans cultures from all over the world.

Angels in national costume from all continents dance together on this colourful banner with its message of hope and guidance.

Throughout Europe, America, Africa, India and Asia, angels or divine spirits still play an important role in most religions and have long been recorded in religious texts, literature and art as friends and guides.

we·should·not·FORGET·to·entertain·strangers
lest·we·entertain·angels·unawares

Angels of the World Banner

This beautiful wall hanging would make a wonderful focal point in a room. Angels from all over the world have been stitched in cross stitch, French knots and backstitch and given extra sparkle and dimension by the use of metallic threads and pretty beads. Instead of being made up as a hanging it could be mounted and framed as a picture.

Stitch count
212 x 128

Design size
38.5 x 23.2cm (15 x 9in)

Materials
14-count Fiddler's Aida in blue, 51 x 35cm (20 x 15in)
★
Size 24 tapestry needle and a beading needle
★
DMC stranded cotton (floss) as listed in chart key
★
Kreinik Very Fine #4 Braid 028 citron
★
Kreinik Blending Filament 032 pearl
★
Mill Hill glass seed beads 02008 light turquoise and 02038 copper
★
Mill Hill petite glass beads 42014 black

1 Prepare for work, referring to Techniques if necessary. Find and mark the centre of the fabric (see page 99) and circle the centre of the chart with a pen. Use an embroidery frame if you wish.

2 Start stitching from the centre of the chart and fabric, using two strands of stranded cotton (floss) for cross stitches and one strand for backstitches. Work all French knots using two strands wound once around the needle.

3 Working in one direction and using one strand of blending filament, overstitch the completed white and DMC 340 cross stitches in the face veil of the second angel from the left. Attach beads where indicated on the chart using a beading needle and matching thread.

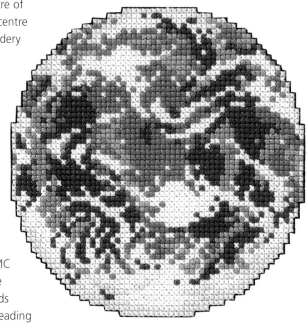

Making Up
Background fabric, 0.5m (½yd)
★
Fusible fleece and fusible web, 0.5m (½yd) each
★
Iron-on interfacing or thin wadding (batting), 0.5m (½yd)
★
Decorative braid, 1.4m (1½yd)
★
Five decorative buttons
★
Permanent fabric glue
★
Dowel, 53.3cm (21in) long

Variations

This design would make a colourful cover for a notebook or diary. Make sure you allow for making up when cutting your fabric. A 28-count evenweave is softer than Aida and easier to wrap around a book.

These angels would also look great sewn or fused as a patch on the front of a large travelling bag. If you want a narrower design, about 18cm (7in) deep, omit the quotation.

Making Up as a Banner

4 Once the stitching is complete, make up the banner as follows. Cut two 54.6 x 40.6cm (21½ x 16in) pieces of background fabric plus three 10 x 15cm (4 x 6in) pieces for tabs. Cut a 54.6 x 40.6cm (21½ x 16in) piece of fusible fleece and fuse this to the wrong side of one of the fabric pieces, following the manufacturer's instructions.

5 Position the embroidery on the right side of the fleece-lined fabric, sewing or fusing it on according to the following instructions. **Applying the embroidery to a background fabric by sewing:** Use the weave of the Aida fabric as a guide to trim to within twelve rows of the design. Fold over the edges by eight rows, leaving four rows showing around the design. Press these folds into place. To avoid the background fabric showing through the embroidery, cut a piece of thin cotton wadding (batting) or felt the same size as the design and insert it behind the embroidery before stitching it down. Place the design and wadding (batting) on the fabric and machine or hand stitch it in place close to the edge, using the fabric weave as a guide.

Applying the embroidery to a background fabric by fusing: Trim and fold the finished embroidery as above. To avoid the background fabric showing through, cut a piece of medium-weight iron-on interfacing the same size as the design and insert it behind the embroidery. Use a press cloth to iron and fuse the pieces together from the wrong side, keeping the folded edges in place. Cut one piece of fusible web the same size as the prepared embroidery. Sandwich the web between the right side of the background fabric and the prepared embroidery, making sure that no edges of fusible web are visible, trimming it if necessary. Pin or tack (baste) in place. Using a press cloth, fuse the layers according to the manufacturer's instructions. *(Continue on page 11.)*

In this dim world of clouding cares,
We rarely know, till 'wildered eyes
see white wings lessening up the skies,
The angels with us unawares.
Gerald Massey (1828–1907),
English poet

we·should·not·forget·to·enter[ta]
lest·we·entertain·angels·u

6 Stitch or glue the length of decorative braid around the outer edge of the embroidery, starting and ending at centre bottom, attaching a decorative button where the ends meet.

7 To make the four tabs, fold each piece of 10 x 15cm (4 x 6in) fabric in half lengthwise, right sides together. Sew a 1.25cm (½in) seam down the length and across one short end. Trim the seam, turn right side out and press. Pin the tabs evenly across the top of the banner, with the sewn ends pointing towards the centre and raw edges matching.

8 Place the second piece of background fabric on top, right side facing, and stitch a 1.25cm (½in) seam all around leaving a gap for turning. Turn right side out, press and slipstitch the gap closed. Bring the loose ends of the tabs to the front and sew on a decorative button at each end. Paint the dowel to complement the embroidery and allow to dry. Insert the dowel through the tabs, ready to hang the banner.

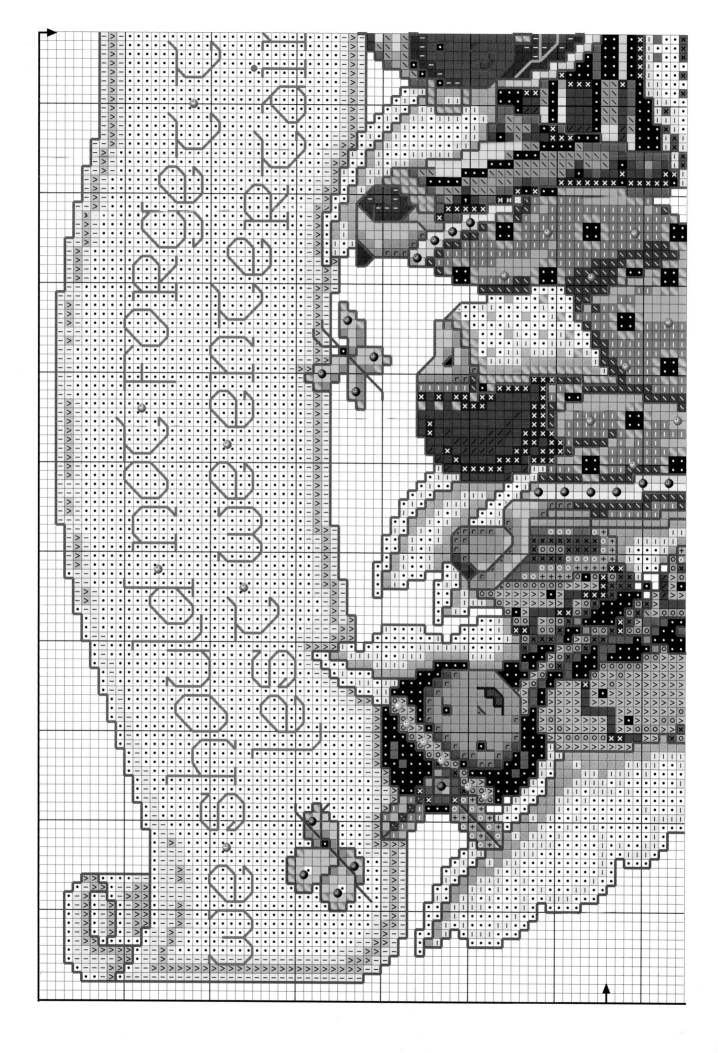

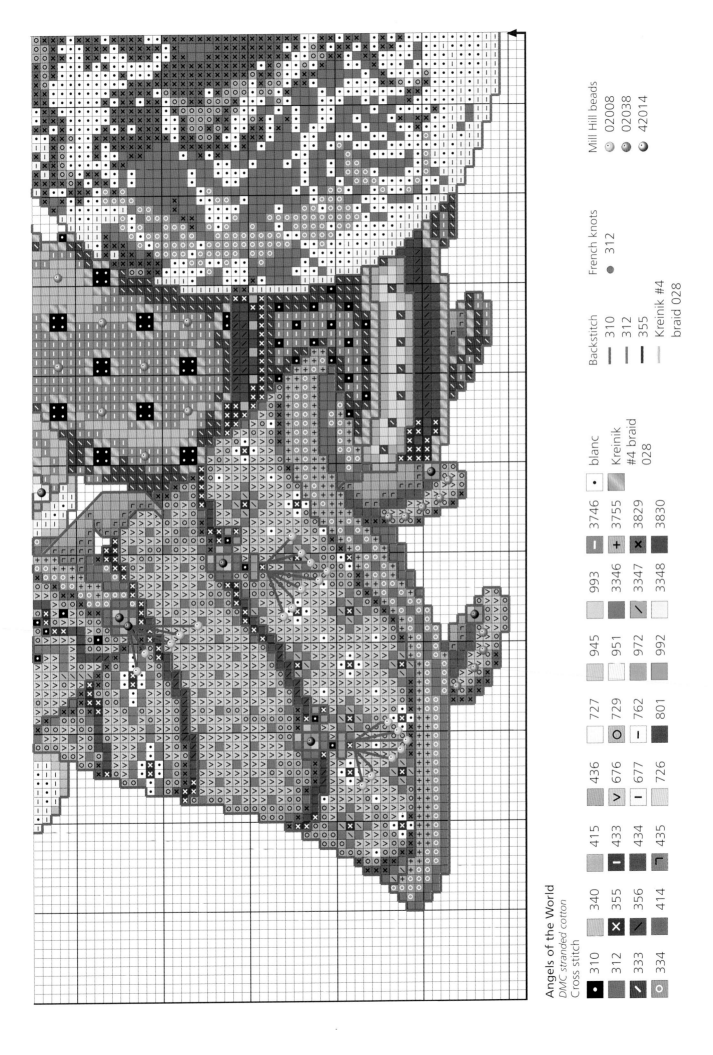

Angels of the World
DMC stranded cotton
Cross stitch

310	340
312	355
333	356
334	414

415	436
433	676
434	677
435	726

727	945
729	951
762	972
801	992

993	3746	blanc
3346	3755	Kreinik
3347	3829	#4 braid
3348	3830	028

Backstitch
— 310
— 312
— 355
— Kreinik #4
    braid 028

French knots
● 312

Mill Hill beads
02008
02038
42014

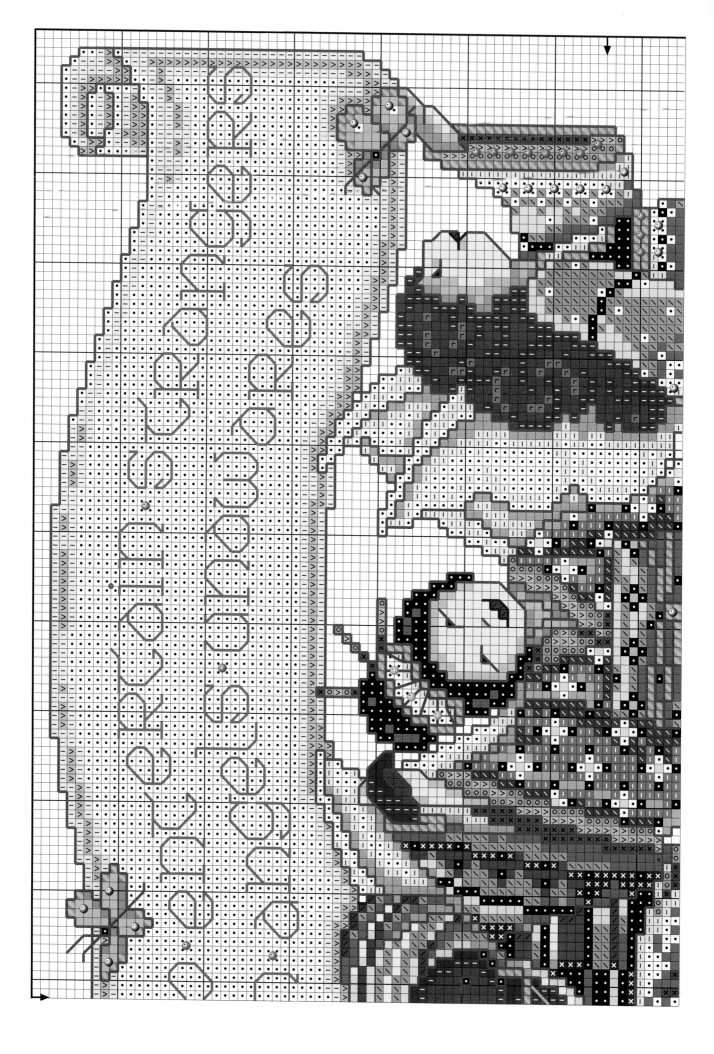

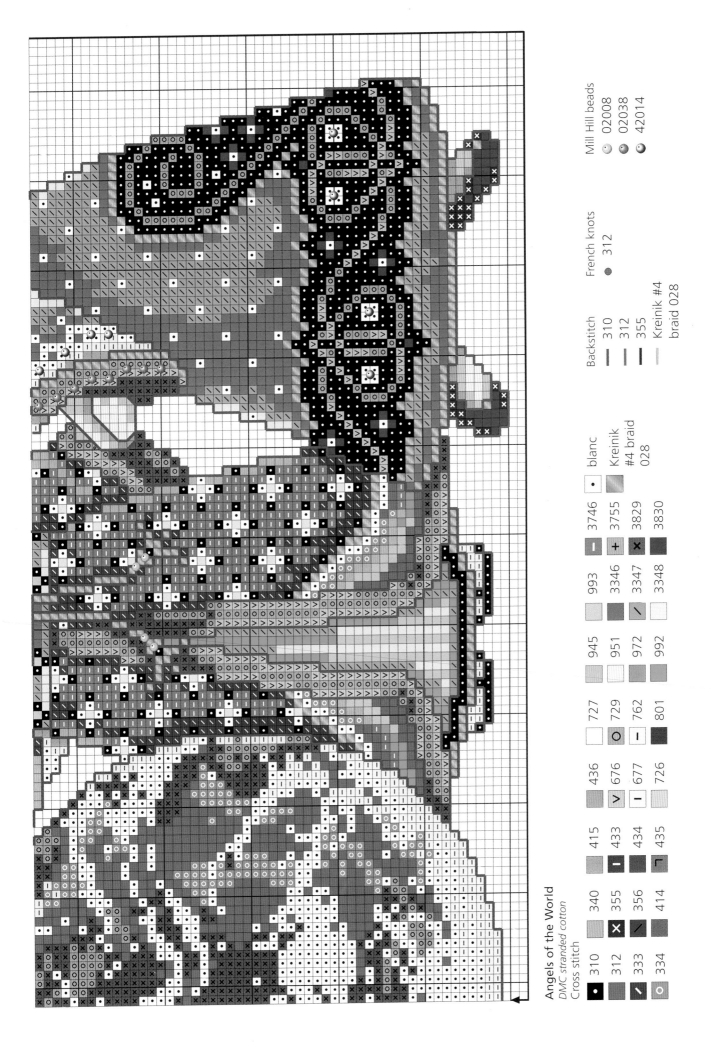

Angels of the World
DMC stranded cotton
Cross stitch

Backstitch
— 310
— 312
— 355
Kreinik #4
braid 028

French knots
● 312

Mill Hill beads
🔘 02008
🔘 02038
🔘 42014

Designed by Claire Crompton

Birthday Angels

The concept of angels with a human face, body and wings is long-established and one that we are very familiar with today. Such images were frequently mentioned in the Old Testament of the Bible, and later religious ideas described angels in even more detail. The serene, other-worldly beauty of angels has become the model celebrated by poets and painters for centuries.

These beautiful designs have a look of archangels about them. Their shining brightness is created in various ways. Each offers a different crystal treasure or charm and the angels are embellished with lustrous beads and gleaming metallic threads, resulting in twelve enchanting and versatile designs.

The angel designs in this chapter combine the traditional winged image of angels with the birthstones and character trait associated with each month.

★ Angel Cards ★

These lovely designs are perfect for birthday cards. Each one is mounted in a hand-made card, with instructions on page 32 showing you how to make them. Using the alphabets on page 33, you could replace the month, gemstone and its meaning with the recipient's name or your own message to create a really special keepsake.

Birthstone – Garnet

January

Throughout history, the deep red of the gemstone, garnet, has represented fire, faith, constancy and fidelity. It was often worn by travellers to light their way at night and protect against evil.

Prepare for work and begin from the centre of the fabric and chart. Work over one block, using two strands of stranded cotton (floss) for cross stitch, one for backstitch and three for blending filament. For tweeded cross stitches (see page 98) use one strand of each colour. Attach beads with a beading needle and matching thread. Personalize the design if you wish using the alphabet on page 33. Make a card (see page 32) and mount the embroidery in it.

Stitch count
59 x 45

Design size
10.7 x 8.2cm (4¼ x 3¼in)

Materials
14-count Aida in cream,
20 x 20cm (8 x 8in)

★

Size 26 tapestry needle
and a beading needle

★

DMC stranded cotton (floss)
as listed in chart key

★

Kreinik Blending Filament
061 ruby

★

Mill Hill glass seed beads
00367

★

Mill Hill crystal treasure
13046, red heart

★

Mauve or ruby pearlized
card with 11.5 x 9cm
(4½ x 3½in) aperture

DMC stranded cotton
Cross stitch

▨ 152	▨ 754	☐ 948	**T** 814 + 514 tweeded	Backstitch	Mill Hill beads
I 223	▨ 814	✕ 3857	**K** Kreinik blending	— 154	◉ 00367
• 225	╱ 815	O 3858	filament 061	— 356	Mill Hill crystal treasure
▨ 498	• 838	− 3859			✦ 13046

February

Amethyst is the royal colour purple and throughout history has been used by monarchs all over the world. It is also a holy colour used by many faiths.

Stitch count
45 x 59

Design size
8.2 x 10.7cm (3¼ x 4¼in)

Materials
28-count evenweave in lilac, 20 x 20cm (8 x 8in)

★

Size 26 tapestry needle and a beading needle

★

DMC stranded cotton (floss) as listed in chart key

★

DMC stranded metallic thread 5284 gold

★

Mill Hill frosted glass beads 62024

★

Mill Hill glass treasure 12017, amethyst rose

★

Purple parchment-effect card with 9 x 11.5cm (3½ x 4½in) aperture

Prepare for work and begin from the centre of the fabric and chart. Work over two threads of evenweave, working cross stitches with two strands of stranded cotton (floss) and backstitches with one strand. For tweeded cross stitches (see page 98) use one strand of each colour. Attach beads with a beading needle and matching thread. Personalize the design if you wish using the alphabet on page 33. Make a card (see page 32) and mount the embroidery in it.

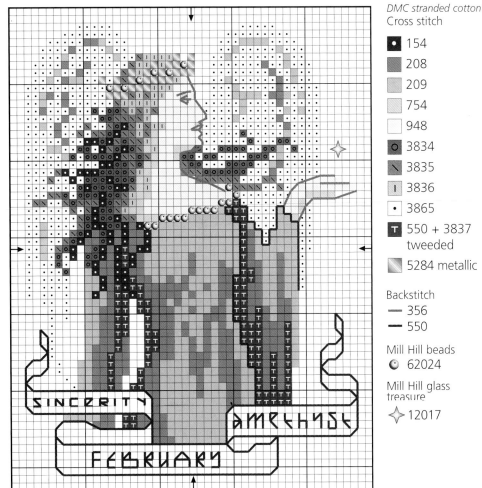

DMC stranded cotton
Cross stitch

●	154
▨	208
▨	209
□	754
□	948
◉	3834
◥	3835
I	3836
·	3865
T	550 + 3837 tweeded
▨	5284 metallic

Backstitch
— 356
— 550

Mill Hill beads
◕ 62024

Mill Hill glass treasure
✦ 12017

Birthstone – Aquamarine

March

Aquamarine literally means sea water, and the gem was thought to contain the spirit of the sea. Legends say that aquamarine was found in the treasure chests of mermaids.

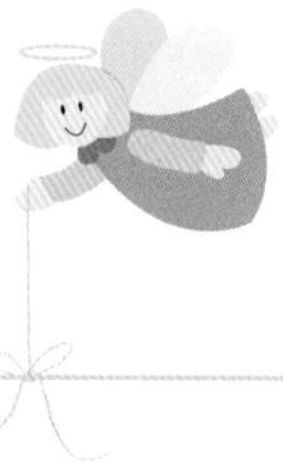

Stitch count
45 x 60

Design size
8.2 x 10.9cm
(3¼ x 4¼in)

Materials
14-count Aida in ice blue, 20 x 20cm (8 x 8in)

★

Size 26 tapestry needle and a beading needle

★

DMC stranded cotton (floss) as listed in chart key

★

Kreinik Blending Filament 014 sky blue

★

Mill Hill glass seed beads 02017

★

Brass charm, sea-horse

★

Blue parchment-effect card with 9 x 11.5cm (3½ x 4½in) aperture

Prepare for work and begin from the centre of the fabric and chart. Work over one block, using two strands of stranded cotton (floss) for cross stitch and one for backstitch. For tweeded cross stitches (see page 98) use one strand each of 747 and 564, and use one strand of 747 with two strands of blending filament. Attach beads with a beading needle and matching thread. Personalize the design if you wish using the alphabet on page 33. Make a card (see page 32) and mount the embroidery in it.

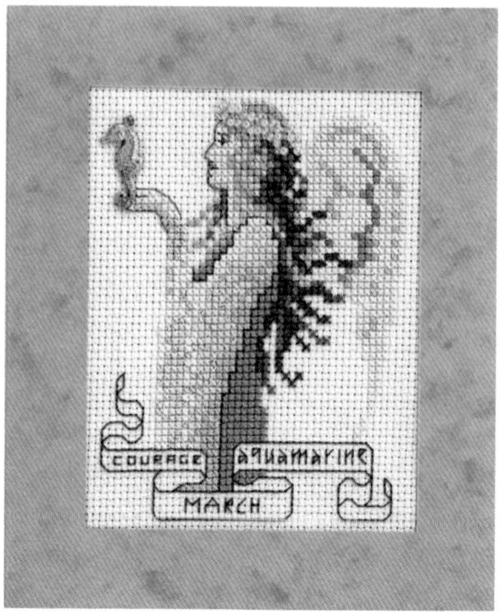

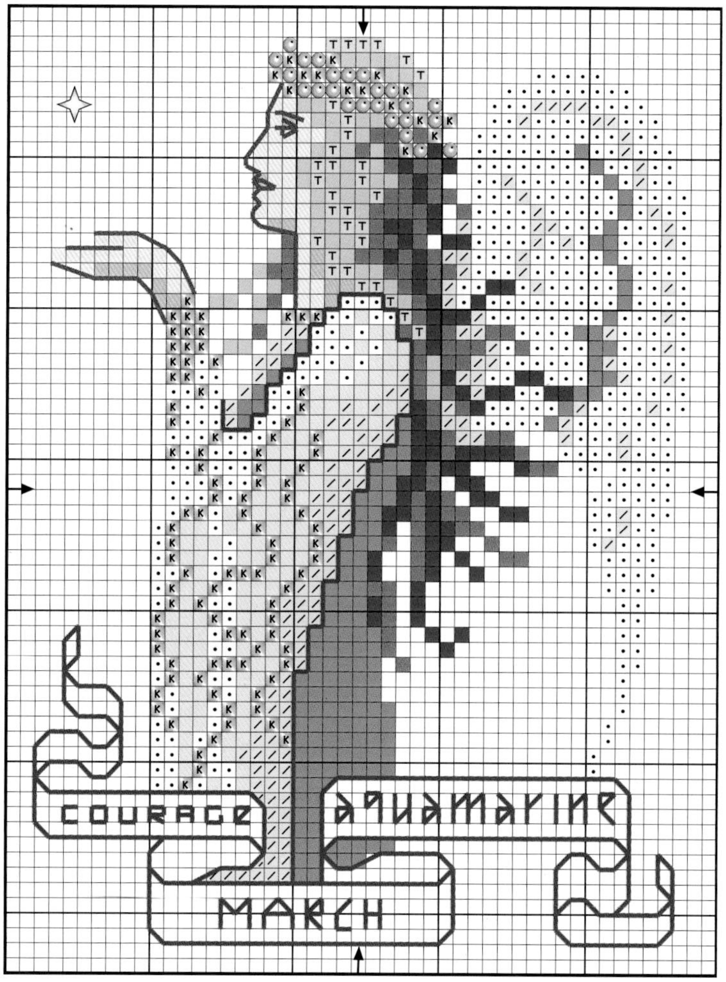

DMC stranded cotton
Cross stitch
- 505
- 562
- 563
- • 747
- 754
- 807
- 948
- 3761
- / 3766
- T 747 + 564 tweeded
- K 747 + Kreinik 014 tweeded

Backstitch
- 356
- 505

Mill Hill beads
- 02017

Brass sea-horse charm

April

Diamonds are the hardest and most brilliant of the gemstones, containing the light of stars and have been prized throughout history. The colour or lustre of a diamond is called its 'water'.

Stitch count
56 x 45

Design size
10 x 8.2cm (4 x 3¼in)

Materials
28-count evenweave in denim blue, 20 x 20cm (8 x 8in)

★

Size 26 tapestry needle and a beading needle

★

DMC stranded cotton (floss) as listed in chart key

★

DMC stranded metallic thread 5272 white

★

Mill Hill glass seed beads 00161

★

Mill Hill crystal bead or diamante stone

★

Lilac parchment-effect card with 11.5 x 9cm (4½ x 3½in) aperture

Prepare for work and begin from the centre of the fabric and chart. Work over two threads of evenweave, using two strands of stranded cotton (floss) for cross stitch and one for backstitch. For tweeded cross stitches (see page 98) use one strand of each colour. Attach beads with a beading needle and matching thread. Personalize the design if you wish using the alphabet on page 33. Make a card (see page 32) and mount the embroidery in it.

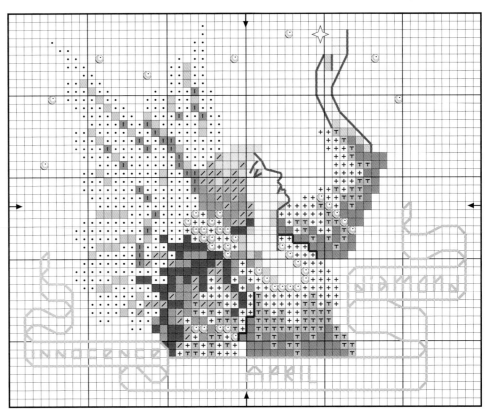

DMC stranded cotton
Cross stitch

▉ 420	◪ 3046	• blanc	
▨ 754	░ 3047	▨ 3839 + 5272 tweeded	
□ 948	I 3839	T 3840 + 5272 tweeded	
▨ 3045	▨ 3840	+ blanc + 5272 tweeded	

Backstitch
— 356
— 796
— blanc

Mill Hill beads
◉ 00161
✧ Crystal bead

Birthstone – Emerald
May

Emerald green is the colour of life and of nature. The Romans dedicated the precious emerald stone to Venus, their goddess of love and beauty.

Prepare for work and begin from the centre of the fabric and chart. Work over two threads of evenweave, using two strands of stranded cotton (floss) for cross stitch and one for backstitch. For tweeded cross stitches (see page 98) use one strand of each colour. Use three strands of blending filament. Attach beads with a beading needle and matching thread. Personalize the design if you wish using the alphabet on page 33. Make a card (see page 32) and mount the embroidery in it.

Stitch count
45 x 58

Design size
8.2 x 10.5cm
(3¼ x 4⅛in)

Materials
28-count evenweave in cream, 20 x 20cm
(8 x 8in)
★
Size 26 tapestry needle and a beading needle
★
DMC stranded cotton (floss) as listed in chart key
★
Kreinik Blending Filament 008 green
★
Mill Hill glass seed beads 02054
★
Mill Hill crystal treasure 13003, 3 emerald flowers (3 in pack)
★
Green card with 9 x 11.5cm (3½ x 4½in) aperture

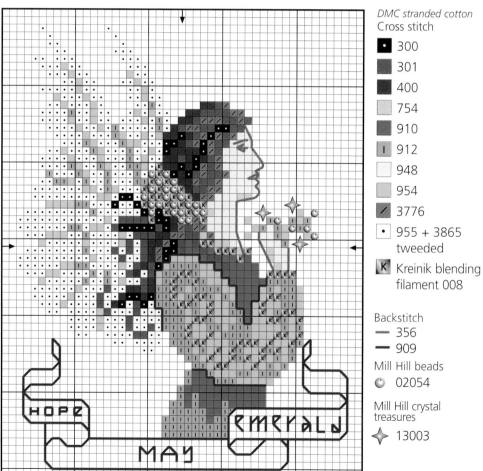

DMC stranded cotton
Cross stitch

■	300
	301
	400
	754
	910
I	912
	948
	954
╱	3776
•	955 + 3865 tweeded
K	Kreinik blending filament 008

Backstitch
— 356
— 909

Mill Hill beads
● 02054

Mill Hill crystal treasures
✦ 13003

June

The Romans believed moonstone to be made from moonlight. Its bluish-white spots of colour do look rather like the surface of the moon when held up to the light.

Prepare for work and begin from the centre of the fabric and chart. Work over two threads of evenweave, using two strands of stranded cotton (floss) for cross stitch and one for backstitch. For tweeded cross stitches (see page 98) use one strand of each colour. Attach beads with a beading needle and matching thread. Personalize the design if you wish using the alphabet on page 33. Make a card (see page 32) and mount the embroidery in it.

Stitch count
45 x 58

Design size
8.2 x 10.5cm (3¼ x 4⅛in)

Materials
28-count evenweave in denim blue, 20 x 20cm (8 x 8in)
★
Size 26 tapestry needle and a beading needle
★
DMC stranded cotton (floss) as listed in chart key
★
DMC stranded metallic thread 5283 silver
★
Mill Hill antique glass beads 03007
★
Mill Hill glass treasure 12184, crescent moon
★
Lilac parchment-effect card with 9 x 11.5cm (3½ x 4½in) aperture

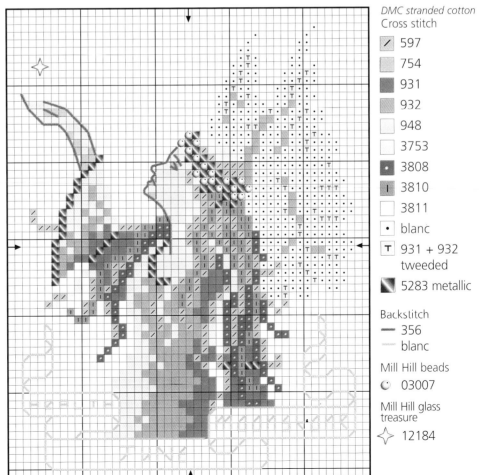

DMC stranded cotton
Cross stitch

∕	597
	754
	931
	932
	948
	3753
•	3808
I	3810
	3811
•	blanc
T	931 + 932 tweeded
◣	5283 metallic

Backstitch
— 356
— blanc

Mill Hill beads
◖ 03007

Mill Hill glass treasure
✧ 12184

Birthstone – Ruby

July

Rubies are often called the king or lord of gemstones, and to be described as
'more precious than rubies' is to be very valuable indeed.

Prepare your fabric for work and begin from the centre of the fabric and centre of the chart. Work over one block of Aida, working cross stitches with two strands of stranded cotton (floss) and backstitches with one strand. For tweeded cross stitches (see page 98) use one strand of each colour. Use three strands of blending filament. Attach beads and the treasure with a beading needle and matching thread. Personalize the design if you wish using the alphabet on page 33. Make a card (see page 32) and mount the embroidery in it.

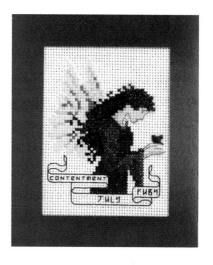

Stitch count
44 x 54

Design size
8 x 9.8cm (3⅛ x 3¾in)

Materials
14-count Aida in cream,
20 x 20cm (8 x 8in)
★
Size 26 tapestry needle
and a beading needle
★
DMC stranded cotton (floss)
as listed in chart key
★
Kreinik Blending Filament
003 red
★
Mill Hill antique glass
beads 03049
★
Mill Hill glass treasure
12050, small red bird
★
Mauve or ruby pearlized
card with 9 x 11.5cm
(3½ x 4½in) aperture

DMC stranded cotton
Cross stitch

◪	300
◪	321
◨	349
▬	356
◨	400
◼	498
◻	754
◼	815
⊙	838
◻	948
⊡	3371
T	225 + 754 tweeded
·	225 + 3865 tweeded
K	Kreinik blending filament 003

Backstitch
— 356
— 814

Mill Hill beads
● 03049

Mill Hill glass treasure
✦ 12050

CONTENTMENT

JULY

RUBY

August

Birthstone – Peridot

Peridot was called the evening emerald by the Romans because its colour did not darken at night. Its yellow-green colour contains the light of the sun and was believed to lighten the shadows of the night.

Stitch count
59 x 45

Design size
10.7 x 8.2cm (4¼ x 3¼in)

Materials
28-count evenweave in cream, 20 x 20cm (8 x 8in)

★

Size 26 tapestry needle and a beading needle

★

DMC stranded cotton (floss) as listed in chart key

★

Kreinik Blending Filament 015 chartreuse

★

Mill Hill glass seed beads 00167

★

Mill Hill glass treasure 12144, 2 medium green leaves (2 in pack)

★

Green card with 11.5 x 9cm (4½ x 3½in) aperture

Prepare your fabric for work and begin from the centre of the fabric and centre of the chart. Work over two threads of evenweave, working cross stitches with two strands of stranded cotton (floss) and backstitches with one strand. Use three strands of blending filament. Attach the beads and the two treasures with a beading needle and matching thread. Personalize the design if you wish using the alphabet on page 33. Make a card (see page 32) and mount the embroidery in it.

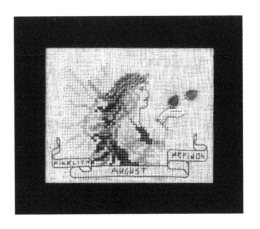

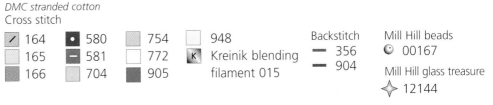

DMC stranded cotton
Cross stitch

✓ 164	● 580	754	948	**Backstitch**	**Mill Hill beads**
165	– 581	772	K Kreinik blending	— 356	◕ 00167
166	704	905	filament 015	— 904	**Mill Hill glass treasure**
					✦ 12144

September

Sapphire is known as the celestial gemstone. According to the ancient Persians, the Earth rests on a sapphire and the sky reflects its deep blue colour.

Stitch count
45 x 56

Design size
8.2 x 10cm (3¼ x 4in)

Materials
14-count Aida in ice blue, 20 x 20cm (8 x 8in)
★
Size 26 tapestry needle and a beading needle
★
DMC stranded cotton (floss) as listed in chart key
★
Kreinik Blending Filament 051HL sapphire hi lustre
★
Mill Hill glass seed beads 02026
★
Mill Hill frosted glass beads 60168
★
Mill Hill glass treasure 12006, sapphire flower
★
Royal blue parchment-effect card with 9 x 11.5cm (3½ x 4½in) aperture

Prepare your fabric for work and begin from the centre of the fabric and centre of the chart. Work over one block of Aida, working cross stitches with two strands of stranded cotton (floss) and backstitches with one strand. For tweeded cross stitches (see page 98) use one strand of each colour. Use three strands of blending filament. Attach beads with a beading needle and matching thread. Personalize the design if you wish using the alphabet on page 33. Make a card (see page 32) and mount the embroidery in it.

DMC stranded cotton
Cross stitch

╱	156
▨	340
▨	341
▨	758
▨	797
▨	800
I	809
▨	904
▨	948
O	3747
·	3865
T	797 + 798 tweeded
K	Kreinik blending filament 051HL

Backstitch
— 356
— 796

Mill Hill beads
◉ 02026
◉ 60168

Mill Hill glass treasure
✦ 12006

Birthstone – Opal

October

The opal is said to be the gemstone of the sky, holding within its centre
rainbows, lightning and the fire of volcanoes.

Prepare your fabric for work and begin from the centre of the fabric and centre of the chart. Work over two threads of evenweave, working cross stitches with two strands of stranded cotton (floss) and backstitches with one strand. For tweeded cross stitches (see page 98) use one strand of each colour. Attach beads with a beading needle and matching thread. Personalize the design if you wish using the alphabet on page 33. Make a card (see page 32) and mount the embroidery in it.

Stitch count
56 x 45

Design size
10 x 8.2cm (4 x 3¼in)

Materials
28-count evenweave in
light blue, 20 x 20cm
(8 x 8in)

★

Size 26 tapestry needle
and a beading needle

★

DMC stranded cotton (floss)
as listed in chart key

★

DMC stranded metallic
thread 5272 white

★

Mill Hill glass seed beads
02017

★

Brass charm, small sun

★

Lilac parchment-effect
card with 11.5 x 9cm
(4½ x 3½in) aperture

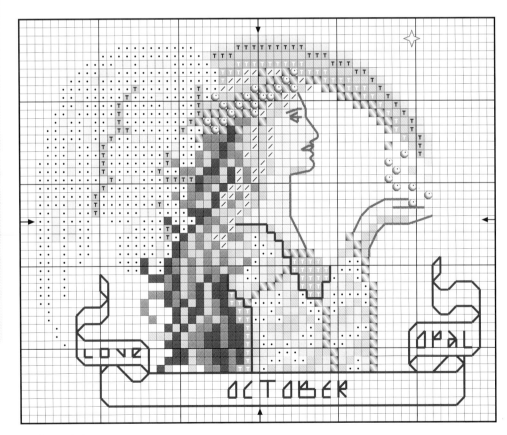

DMC stranded cotton
Cross stitch

					Backstitch	Mill Hill beads
■ 420	□ 948	▨ 3046	**T** 519 + 995 tweeded		— 356	◉ 02017
□ 519	□ 955	╱ 3047	**T** 913 + 995 tweeded		— 797	✧ Brass sun charm
□ 754	▦ 3045	• 3865	▨ 5272 metallic			

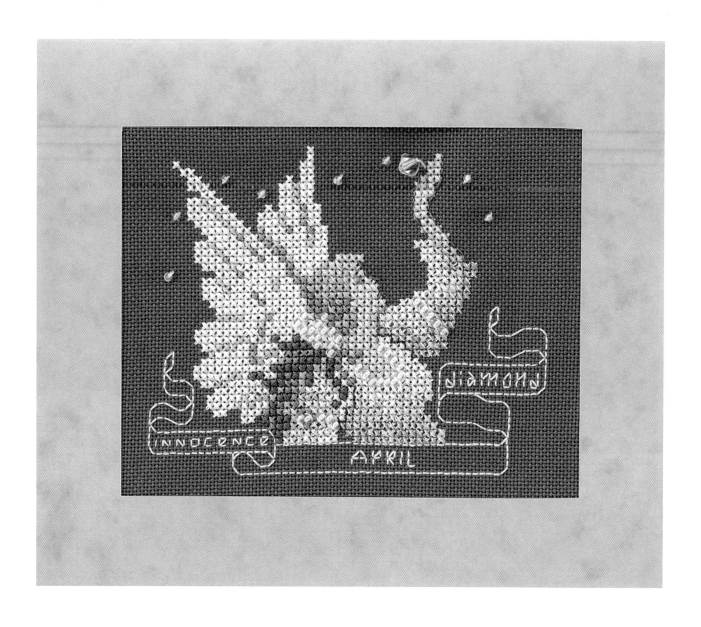

Variations

To create really memorable cards you could
further embellish them using a variety of craft
items and effects such as ribbons, bows, beads,
charms, raffia, handmade paper, stencils,
stamping and paint effects.

Each of the designs would make beautiful little
pictures – a set of four in matching frames would
make a lovely grouping on a wall.

Making an Aperture Card

1 Choose a card colour to complement your
embroidery. Cut a piece of card 39.9 x
15.9cm (15¾ x 6¼in) – see diagram page 33.
On the wrong side of the card, draw two
lines dividing it into three sections of 13.3cm
(5¼in). Score gently along each line with the
back of a craft knife to make folding easier.

2 In the centre section, mark an aperture
8.9 x 11.5cm (3½ x 4½in), leaving a
border of 2.2cm (⅞in) on all sides. Cut out
the aperture with a sharp craft knife, carefully
cutting into the corners neatly. Trim the left
edge of the first section by 2mm (⅛in) so that
it lies flat when folded over to the inside of
the card. This will cover the back of the
stitching. Fold the left and then the right
section on the scored lines.

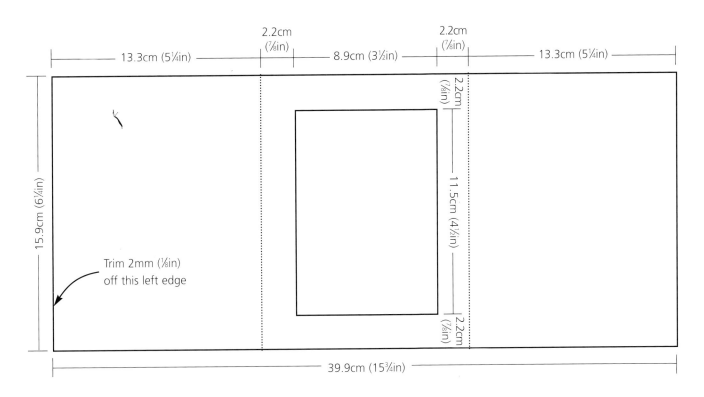

Mounting Embroidery into a Card

1 Lay the card right side up on top of the design so the stitching is in the middle of the aperture. Place a pin in each corner and remove the card. Trim the fabric to within about 1.5cm (⅝in) so it fits into the card.

2 On the wrong side of the card, stick double-sided tape around the aperture and peel off the backing tape. Place the card over the design, using the pins to guide it into position. Press down firmly so the fabric is stuck securely to the card.

3 On the wrong side of the card, stick more double-sided tape around the edge of the middle section. Peel off the backing tape and fold the left section in to cover the back of the stitching, pressing down firmly.

...trimmed and embellished
with scent and sparkle,
all of glowing substance,
without the slightest flaw.
Ch'u Tz'u

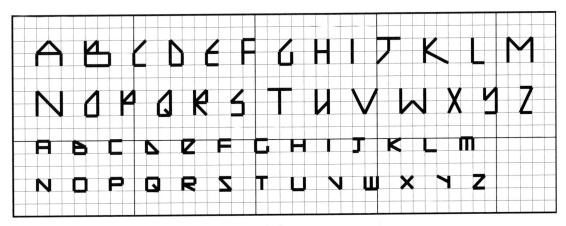

Personalize your cards with these backstitch alphabets

Designed by Sue Cook

Little Angels

Since ancient times societies have believed in spiritual guardians and have prayed to the spirit world to watch over and protect their young. The idea that angels, being close to God, are on hand to protect the vulnerable and innocent here on earth is a powerful one and it isn't surprising that their caring nature and protective abilities are sought. Artists and poets over the centuries have portrayed angels as symbols of purity, innocence and love – attributes we often associate with babies and young children too.

Welcome a new baby with a charming collection of designs – a sampler and card to celebrate the arrival and a door hanger hoping for peaceful nights for the little angel.

Angel Birth Sampler

A heartfelt prayer forms the inspiration for this birth sampler filled with cuddly nursery toys. The design can be stitched on Aida as shown or over two threads of 28-count linen – in either fabric a perfect celebration of the name and birth date of your little angel.

1 Prepare your fabric for work, finding and marking the centre (see page 99). Begin working from the centre of the fabric and the centre of the chart on pages 37 and 38.

2 Stitch over one block of Aida, using two strands for full cross stitches and three-quarter cross stitches and one strand for backstitches.

3 Use the alphabet on page 43 to personalize your sampler. Carefully draw your child's name and birth date on graph paper and count the number of squares it uses (including spaces as well). Count the number of squares in the space provided and centre the name and date. If you are using this as a birth sampler for twins, or you have a longer name to fit in, you may wish to omit the verse.

4 When all the stitching is complete, carefully wash and iron your work if necessary and prepare for mounting and framing (see framing a sampler on page 46).

Stitch count
132 x 99

Design size
24 x 18cm (9½ x 7in)

Materials
14-count Aida in cream, 38 x 33cm (15 x 13in)

★

Size 26 tapestry needle

★

DMC stranded cotton (floss) as listed in chart key

★

Graph paper and pencil

★

Frame and mount of your choice

A baby is an angel whose wings decrease as his legs increase.

(French proverb)

Angel Birth Sampler
DMC stranded cotton
Cross stitch

209	598	• 838	3853
∧ 210	O 739	956	+ 3854
⌐ 341	\ 742	/ 957	3855
433	× 743	I 3747	• blanc
435	744	– 3771	
437	– 746	/ 3810	Backstitch
453	754	3839	▬ 838
597	V 818	3840	

May Angels
watch you
night & day
as you sleep
& as you play

SAMUEL JAMES
CHORLEY
2nd MAY 2003

Angel Birth
Sampler
DMC stranded cotton
Cross stitch

	209
∧	210
⌐	341
	433
	435
	437
	453
	597
	598
O	739
\	742
×	743
	744
−	746
	754
V	818
⊙	838
	956
/	957
I	3747
−	3771
/	3810
	3839
	3840
	3853
+	3854
	3855
•	blanc

Backstitch
— 838

Sleepy Angel Door Hanger

This design (shown on page 41) makes a charming door sign to keep the household quiet when the little one is asleep. The winged horse would also look very attractive framed as a picture for a nursery wall.

Stitch count
100 x 83

Design size
18 x 15cm (7⅛ x 6in)

Materials
14-count Aida in cream,
33 x 30cm (13 x 12in)
★
Size 26 tapestry needle
★
DMC stranded cotton (floss)
as listed in chart key
★
White card, 20 x 18cm
(8 x 7in)
★
Wadding (batting),
20 x 18cm (8 x 7in)
★
Felt, 20 x 18cm (8 x 7in)
★
Gold ribbon, 6mm wide
x 20cm (8in) long
★
Pre-gathered broderie
anglaise, 1m (1yd)
★
Clear glue
★
Double-sided
adhesive tape

1 Prepare your fabric for work, beginning stitching from the centre of the fabric and chart on page 40. Stitch over one block of Aida, using two strands for full cross stitches and three-quarter cross stitches and one strand for backstitches. You could change the colour of the wording and star wings depending on whether the design is for a boy or girl.

Making Up the Door Hanger

2 To make the door hanger, cover one side of the white card with strips of double-sided tape. Lay the wadding (batting) on a flat surface and press the taped side of the card on top. Trim excess wadding to neaten. Place your stitching centrally on top of the wadding (batting) counting about five squares from the top and bottom border and seven squares from the side borders. Fold the fabric to the back using the edges of the card to form sharp creases. It is important to have the same number of squares around all edges or your design will look crooked. Using the creases as a guide, use double-sided tape to secure the fabric to the back.

Stick long edges first, from the centre outwards and keep checking the front to ensure you are not pulling the straight edges out of line. Trim fabric at the corners to make them easier to fold.

3 Neaten one edge of the broderie anglaise by folding over and securing with a spot of glue. Beginning at the middle of the bottom edge, spread glue lightly on the card and allow it to become tacky before sticking the trimming on, following the edge as closely as possible. Using pre-gathered trimming makes it simpler to form neat corners. Continue around all the edges and secure neatly at the back, overlapping the point where you started to avoid a gap.

4 To make a ribbon hanging loop, measure in 5cm (2in) from the sides on the back of the hanger and make pencil marks. Secure the ribbon to the marks using double-sided tape, first ensuring that the sign will hang straight. For a neat finish stick a piece of felt or thin card to the back.

Hush, my dear, lie still and slumber
holy angels guard thy bed,
Heavenly blessings without number
gently falling on thy head.
Cradle hymn,
Isaac Watts (1674–1748)

Sleepy Angel Door Hanger
DMC stranded cotton
Cross stitch

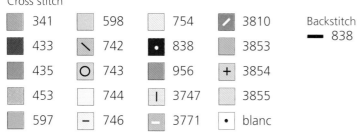

341	598	754	3810	Backstitch
433	742	838	3853	— 838
435	743	956	3854	
453	744	3747	3855	
597	746	3771	blanc	

Designed by Lesley Teare

Wedding Angel

Angels have long been depicted as symbols of love, beauty and purity and a bride on her wedding day epitomizes all these qualities, particularly in Western tradition.

The sight of a radiant young woman at her most beautiful, dressed in gauzy white, a trailing veil for wings and a headdress for a halo, brings angels to mind, those icons of divine perfection. And what woman doesn't want to be called an angel, to be seen as far above the norm – even for just a day?

This beautiful design is the epitome of all that is romantic in a wedding with a sweet angel-bride almost floating on air with happiness.

Wedding Sampler

A magical sparkle is created in this atmospheric design by the use of metallic threads among the delicately coloured stranded cotton (floss) shades, making this a sampler that is sure to become a treasured memento. The names and date featured are easily changed using the charted backstitch alphabet provided.

Stitch count
177 x 139

Design size
32 x 25.2cm (12½ x 10in)

Materials
28-count Quaker linen in biscuit 51 x 45.5cm (20 x 18in)

★

Size 26 tapestry needle

★

DMC stranded cotton (floss) as listed in chart key

★

DMC Art 273 metallic thread

★

Kreinik Very Fine (#4) Braid, gold 002HL

★

Suitable picture frame

★

Mount board

★

Wadding (batting)

★

Double-sided adhesive tape

★

Pins

★

Crochet cotton or strong thread

1 Prepare the fabric for work, finding and marking the centre (see page 99). Mount the fabric in an embroidery frame if you wish. Begin stitching from the centre of the fabric and the centre of the chart on pages 48–51.

2 Work over two linen threads, using two strands of stranded cotton (floss) for full cross stitches and three-quarter cross stitches and one strand for backstitches and French knots (with the thread wrapped twice around the needle). Use one strand of metallic thread for cross stitches and backstitches. Because of the number of colour changes it is a good idea to keep several needles threaded with each colour.

3 Complete the angel before working the ornate brackets. Take great care in counting the squares and if in any doubt run a line of tacking (basting) stitches to show the correct distance. Change the names and date using the charted alphabet on page 49, using one strand of stranded cotton (floss) for the backstitch.

4 When all the stitching is complete, remove from the frame, press the sampler carefully and then frame.

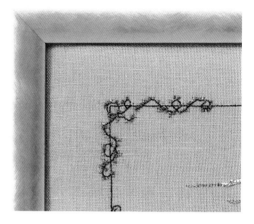

Framing the Sampler

5 Cut your mount board to the size of the picture frame aperture. Cut a piece of wadding (batting) the same size and secure to the board with double-sided tape.

6 Lay your embroidery face up on the wadding (batting) and when you are happy with the position, push a line of pins down each side into the board. Check the stitching is straight then trim the fabric to leave 5cm (2in) all round.

7 Fold the excess fabric to the back. Thread a needle with a long length of crochet cotton or strong thread, knot the end and lace the two opposite sides together on the back, starting at one end and working in an under-and-over motion. When you reach the other end, adjust the laced threads one by one before finishing off. Repeat this process on the two remaining edges.

8 Fold down the corners and stitch neatly in place. Remove the pins and put your work in its frame.

Variations

Stitch just the ornate brackets, either as a pair or arranged as a full border, to decorate a wedding card with your own message.

Stitch other parts of the design, such as the dove or a spray of flowers, to decorate a bridesmaid's gift bag.

To love for the sake of being loved is human, but to love for the sake of loving is angelic.

Alphonse de Lamartine (1790–1869), French poet and historian

Designed by Joan Elliott

Angel House Rules

The many virtues of angels are well described in religious writings, in literature and art, and their perfect, flawless nature that many believe in is nowadays given far more attention than the more fierce and judgemental characteristics described in the Bible. Today, to 'be an angel' means to be thoughtful, kind and loving, to consider others and to play our part in ensuring smooth relations in an often stressful world.

Angels are often described as god's divine assistants and as such they are associated with higher nature, with altruistic love, peace, fulfilment and joy. This joyful design is intended to bring a smile, to be a gentle reminder that we can emulate the best qualities of angels in even the smallest of ways.

Stitch this cherubic version of the ever-popular 'house rules' and encourage every family member to 'be an angel' and lend a hand.

52

Be an Angel
...and...
Help Stay Up
Take Down a Message
Put Away Your Things
Scrub It All Clean
Be Kind To Your Friends
Remember To Share
and Always Give Thanks for Each Day

Be an Angel Banner

This utterly charming cross stitch design is a humorous reminder for all the family to play their part in ensuring the household runs peacefully and smoothly. Many of the small scenes that make up the hanging could be stitched separately as little pictures or cards.

Stitch count
113 x 323

Design size
20.5 x 58.5cm (8 x 23in)

Materials
14-count Aida in antique white, 33 x 71cm (13 x 28in)

★

Size 24 tapestry needle

★

DMC stranded cotton (floss) as listed in chart key

★

Background fabric, 0.5m (½yd)

★

Fusible fleece, 0.5m (½yd)

★

Iron-on interfacing or thin wadding (batting), 0.25m (¼yd)

★

Fusible web, 0.25m (¼yd)

★

Decorative braid to tone with embroidery, 1.8m (2yd)

★

Four decorative buttons

★

Permanent fabric glue

★

Dowel painted to tone with embroidery, 29cm (11½in) length

1 Prepare for work, referring to page 99 of Techniques if necessary. Find and mark the centre of the fabric and circle the centre of the chart with a pen. Use an embroidery frame if you wish. Start stitching from the centre of the chart and fabric, using two strands of stranded cotton (floss) for full cross stitches and three-quarter stitches and one for backstitches. Work all French knots using two strands wound once around the needle.

Making Up as a Banner

2 Once the embroidery is complete, make up the banner as follows. Cut two 32 x 70cm (12½ x 27½in) pieces of background fabric plus three 10 x 15cm (4 x 6in) pieces for tabs. Cut a 32 x 70cm (12½ x 27½in) piece of fusible fleece and fuse this to the wrong side of one of the fabric pieces, following the manufacturer's instructions. Now position the embroidery on the right side of the fleece-lined fabric, sewing or fusing it in position according to the instructions on page 9, step 5.

3 Using matching sewing thread, stitch (or glue) the length of decorative braid around the outer edge of the embroidery, starting and ending at centre bottom, sewing on one of the buttons where the ends meet.

We are each of us angels with only one wing, and we can only fly by embracing each other.
Luciano de Crescenzo,
Italian actor/director

4 To make the tabs, fold each piece of 10 x 15cm (4 x 6in) fabric in half lengthwise, right sides together. Sew a 1.25cm (½in) seam down the length and across one short end. Trim the seam, turn right side out and press. Now place and pin the tabs evenly across the top of the banner with sewn ends pointing towards centre and raw edges matching.

5 Place the second piece of background fabric on top with right side facing and stitch a 1.25cm (½in) seam all around leaving a gap for turning. Turn right side out, press and slipstitch the gap closed. Bring the loose ends of the tabs to the front and sew on a decorative button at each end. Insert the length of dowel through the tabs, ready to hang the banner.

310	318	334	415	434	436	437	597	598	676	677	726	727	729	743	746	747	762	797	801	869	945	951	3325	3346

Be an Angel

DMC stranded cotton

Cross stitch

| 310 | 318 | 334 | 415 | 434 | 436 | 437 | 597 | 598 | 676 | 677 | 726 | 727 | 729 | 743 | 746 | 747 | 762 | 797 | 801 | 869 | 945 | 951 | 3325 | 3346 |

Designed by Lesley Teare

Angel Alphabet

Angels have been thought by many societies throughout history to accompany us from birth through life, acting as personal guides and guardians. In Islamic belief, each person is thought to have two pairs of *hafaza*, acting as guardians for that individual, day and night. In Jewish tradition too everyone has a guardian angel assigned to them at birth.

Stitch your own protective angels to watch over you and your family with this delightful alphabet which has a different flower-decked little angel for each letter, all in a charming Victorian style.

You are sure to find many uses for this wonderful alphabet, such as the little picture, card and trinket pot shown here.

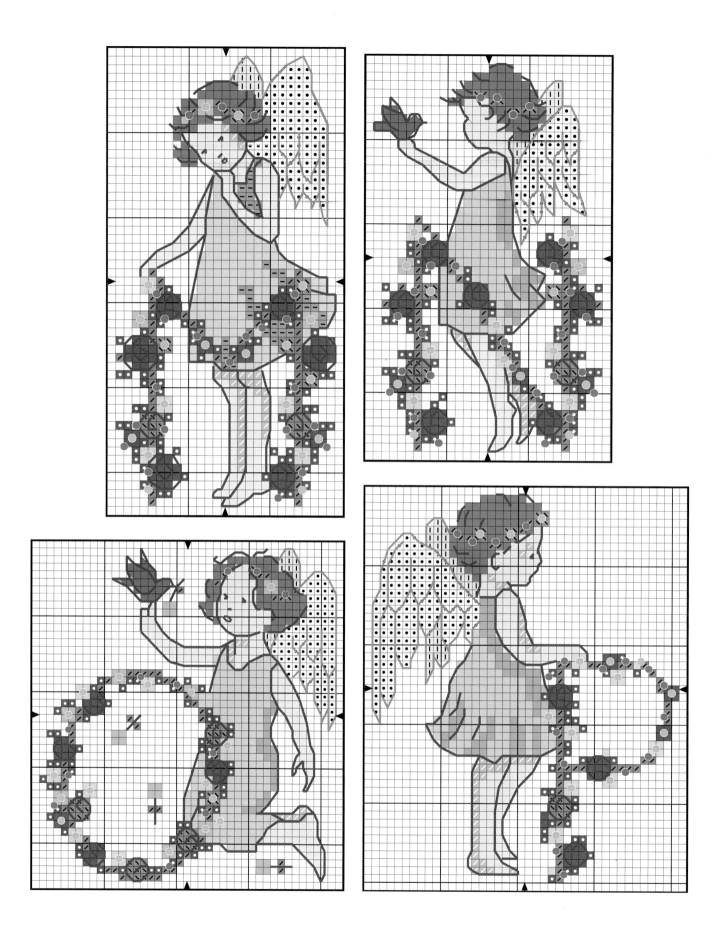

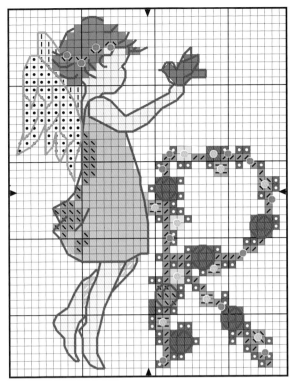

DMC stranded cotton
Cross stitch

164	760	948	I ecru	
167	761	988	• blanc	
642	772	3328	French knots	
676	— 807	3766	○ 738	
754	● 895	3842	● 3842	

Backstitch
— 783
— 801
— 3328

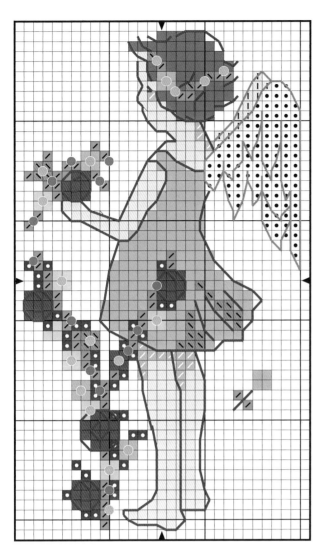

DMC stranded cotton
Cross stitch

				Backstitch
▨ 164	◪ 760	▨ 948	⊡ ecru	▬ 783
▨ 167	▨ 761	◪ 988	⊡ blanc	▬ 801
▨ 642	▨ 772	▨ 3328	French knots	▬ 3328
▨ 676	▬ 807	▨ 3766	● 738	
◪ 754	◪ 895	▨ 3842	● 3842	

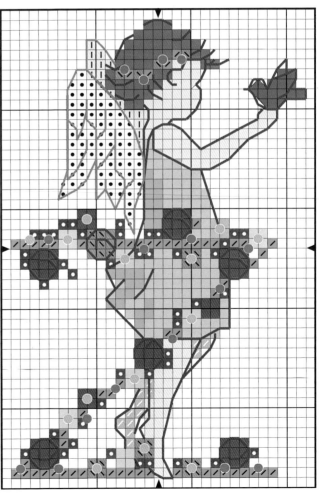

Designed by Helen Philipps

Hobby Angels

Some people believe that angelic influence can encourage us to live life to the fullest, bringing a spiritual dimension that enhances our day-to-day activities. Some of the greatest poets, writers and artists claim to have been touched, directly or indirectly, by divine inspiration when creating their masterpieces.

Appreciation of a job well done or a special skill is always welcome and these charming designs are sure to please friends and family.

We may not all be Shakespeare or da Vinci but even the simplest craft can be made special if it is touched by joy in the making.

Designed by Maria Diaz

Christmas Angels

It is hard to imagine Christmas without angels: from the Angel of the Lord announcing the Nativity in Bethlehem to the angel on the top of the Christmas tree, they are an inseparable part of the festive celebrations.

The angels in this chapter are in two different guises but both styles are absolutely perfect for Christmas time. There are traditional music-playing angels in rich festive colours and sweet, fairy-style angels having fun in the snow. The charts, filled with angels, borders and other festive motifs, are presented in a collage style and can be used in many ways to make a wide range of fabulous Christmas projects.

An angel on an organza bag makes a lovely Christmas gift. Mix and match the angels and borders in this chapter for a wealth of other ideas.

	157
	347
Z	502
\	562
←	712
U	738
	760
	793
	822
↑	3328
	3770
	3799
	3816
	3817
	3863
×	3864
+	blanc
	5282 metallic

Backstitch and long stitch

—	304
—	407
—	414
—	3799
—	5282 metallic

Blue Angel Ornament

The darling little angels in this section are full of fun, and the blue and white theme is perfect for all sorts of Christmas gifts and decorations. Any of the angels could be used to create a pretty hanging for the Christmas tree. The stars could be worked alone for smaller ornaments.

Stitch count
(for motif shown) 58 x 62

Design size
10.5 x 11.2cm (4⅛ x 4½in)

Materials
14-count Aida in navy,
18 x 18cm (7 x 7in)

★

Size 26 tapestry needle

★

DMC stranded cotton (floss)
as listed in chart key

★

DMC stranded metallic
thread as listed in
chart key

★

Stiff card, 18 x 18cm
(7 x 7in)

★

White felt, 18 x 18cm
(7 x 7in)

★

Thin wadding (batting),
18 x 18cm (7 x 7in)

★

Silver cord, 20cm
(8in) long

★

Fabric glue

★

Pinking shears

1 Prepare your fabric for work, marking the centre (see page 99). Begin working from the centre of the motif charted on page 97. If you choose a different motif you will need to check the stitch count and calculate the design size in order to use the correct amount of fabric – see page 99. (The sizes of the card, felt and wadding (batting) used may also need to be altered.)

2 Stitch over one block of Aida, using two strands for cross stitches and one strand for backstitches and straight stitches.

Making Up the Ornament
3 Once the embroidery is complete, make up into a tree hanging. These instructions describe a circular hanging but you could create different shapes (see picture above). Cut a circle from stiff card about 11.5cm (4½in) diameter and one from wadding (batting). Cut another circle a little larger from felt, using pinking shears for a decorative edge.

4 Trim the stitched motif to a circle about 18cm (7in) diameter and stitch a line of loose tacking (basting) all round the edge. Place the embroidery face down, position the wadding (batting) on top, then the card. Fold the embroidery fabric over the card and gather up the tacking (basting) thread tightly.

5 Make a hanging loop from silver cord, stitching or gluing it to the back of the hanging. For a neat finish, glue the felt circle to the back of the hanging.

Variations

Make a festive table runner by scattering all the blue angel designs along a length of linen or Aida fabric. Stars or snowflakes could be stitched around the sides as a border, leaving room for a simple turned hem. Decide what size you want your runner to be and plan the design on graph paper first.

For more rigid ornaments, work the various designs on plastic canvas. Cut out the embroidered designs one square out all round and back with felt for a neat finish. Try different shapes too – hearts and stars would work well.

Blue Angel Card

A whole collection of Christmas cards could be created using some of the many designs in this chapter. Use just one of the angels as shown here or mix and match for a unique look.

1 Prepare your fabric for work, finding and marking the centre (see page 99). Begin working from the centre of the motif from the chart on page 96. If you choose a different motif you will need to check the stitch count and calculate the design size in order to use the correct size of fabric and card – see page 99.

2 Stitch over one block of Aida, using two strands for cross stitches and one strand for backstitches and long straight stitches.

3 Press your design and trim to size for your chosen card mount. Place strips of double-sided tape around the inside of the card aperture. With the embroidery face up, press the card on to the Aida, with the design centrally within the aperture. You could also make your own card – see page 32.

If some people really see angels where others see only empty space, let them paint the angels...
John Ruskin (1819–1900),
English writer and critic

Stitch count
(for motif shown) 38 x 55

Design size
7 x 10cm (2¾ x 4in)

Materials
14-count silver Lurex Aida, 14 x 19cm (5½ x 7½in)
★
Size 26 tapestry needle
★
DMC stranded cotton (floss) as listed in chart key
★
DMC stranded metallic thread as listed in chart key
★
Lilac card blank with 9 x 14cm (3½ x 5½in) oval aperture
★
Double-sided adhesive tape

Variations

Why not stitch a selection of motifs from this chapter and use them to decorate a Christmas sack? Stitch the designs over two threads of a 28-count linen, fray the edges of the patches after the embroidery is complete to give a rustic look and then sew them on to a large ready-made bag.

Create wonderfully festive napkins using the blue angels. Stitch them on rectangles of 28-count linen and then hem the edges. The smaller angels could be stitched and mounted into coasters.

Stitch a pretty cot blanket for a new baby over two threads of an 18-count Afghan evenweave fabric using some of the blue angel designs.

Blue Angel Cake Band

Even a shop-bought Christmas cake will look homemade with this pretty cake band.
It is quick to stitch on a ready-made Aida band, or over two threads of a 28-count linen
band. For a wider cake band use a 9cm (3½in) wide 14-count Aida band and work
the dark blue medium-sized angel charted on page 96.

Design size
4.5cm (1¾in) wide x as
long as required

Materials
16-count white Aida
band, 5.5cm (2¼in) wide
x as long as required
★
Size 26 tapestry needle
★
DMC stranded cotton (floss)
as listed in chart key
★
DMC stranded metallic
thread as listed in
chart key

1 Measure the circumference of
your cake tin to calculate how
long your band needs to be,
allowing an extra 2.5cm (1in) at either
end for hemming later.

2 Begin working about 2.5cm (1in) from
one end of the band, stitching the little
blue angels and stars charted on page 97,
repeating the designs as many times as
required. Stitch over one block of Aida, using
two strands for cross stitches and one strand
for backstitches and long straight stitches.

3 Once all the embroidery is complete, hem
the ends of the Aida band and press
carefully with a cool iron. Pin in place around
your cake.

Outside the open window
the morning air
is all awash with angels.
Richard Purdy Wilbur,
American poet

Variation

The little angel designs, the lines of stars and the
snowflakes charted on pages 96 and 97 could all
be stitched on Aida or linen bands to decorate
towels for Christmas time.

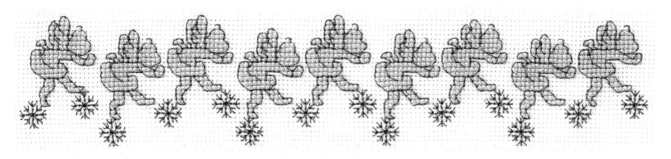

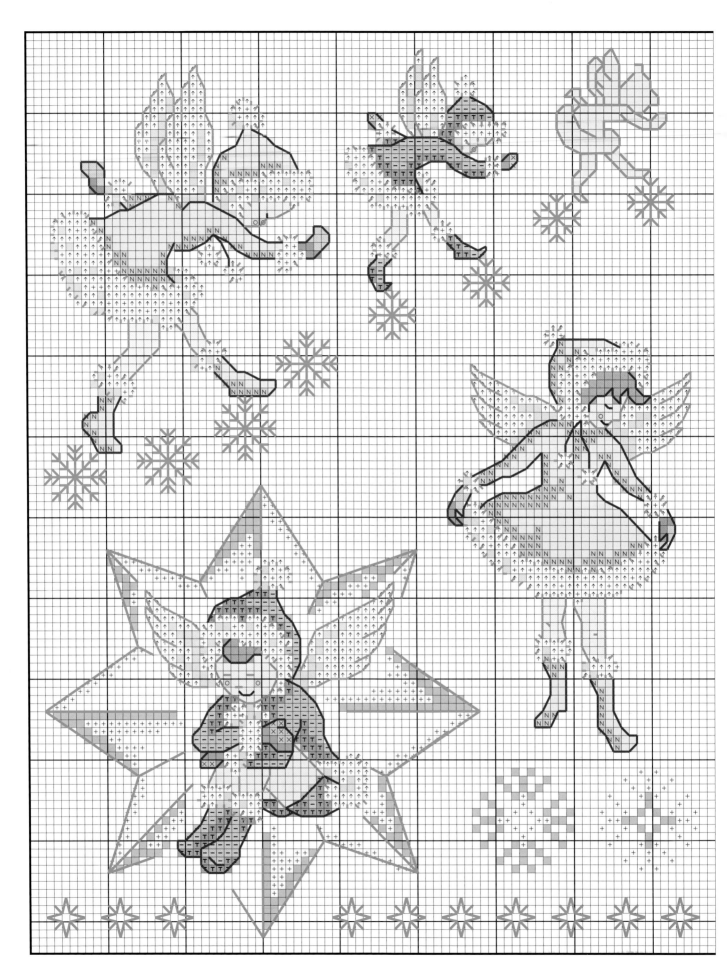

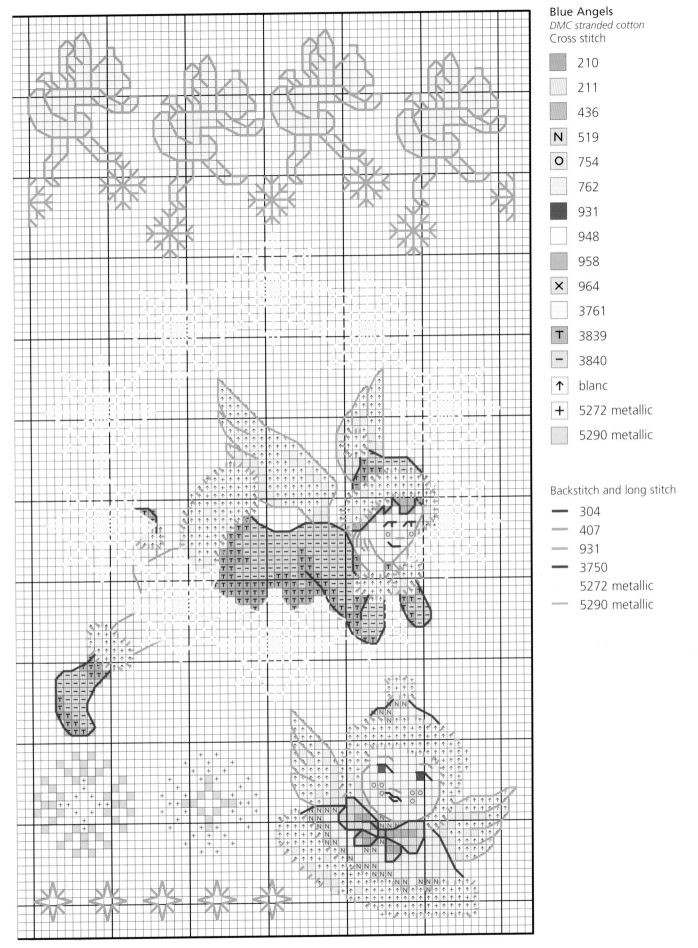

	210
	211
	436
N	519
O	754
	762
	931
	948
	958
×	964
	3761
T	3839
−	3840
↑	blanc
+	5272 metallic
	5290 metallic

Backstitch and long stitch

—	304
—	407
—	931
—	3750
	5272 metallic
—	5290 metallic

Equipment and Techniques

This short but useful section describes the equipment and materials you will need for cross stitch embroidery and the basic techniques and stitches required to work the projects in this book. For beginners there are some handy tips on perfect stitching.

Equipment

Very little equipment is needed for successful cross stitching, which is one of the reasons it's so popular!

Fabrics

The fabrics used for counted cross stitch, mainly Aidas and evenweaves, are woven so they have the same number of threads or blocks to 2.5cm (1in) in both directions. They are available in different thread counts – the higher the count, the more threads or stitches to 2.5cm (1in), and the finer the fabric.

Aida This is ideal for the beginner because the threads are woven in blocks rather than singly. It is available in many fibres, colours and counts and as different width bands. When stitching on Aida, one block on the fabric corresponds to one square on a chart and generally cross stitch is worked over *one block*.

Evenweaves These are made from linen, cotton, acrylic, viscose, modal and mixtures of all of these, are woven singly and are also available in different colours, counts and bands. To even out any oddities in the weave, cross stitch is usually worked over *two threads* of the fabric.

Threads

The most commonly used thread for counted embroidery is stranded cotton (floss) but there are many other types of thread available. Many of the projects in this book feature metallic threads and blending filaments to create extra sparkle. The project instructions give how many strands of each thread to use.
Tweeding You can increase the number of thread colours in your palette by blending or tweeding threads – that is, combining two or more thread colours in the needle at the same time and working as one to achieve a mottled effect.

Tools

There are many tools and gadgets available for embroidery in craft shops but you really only need the following.
Needles Use blunt tapestry needles for cross stitch. The most common sizes used are 24 and 26 but the size depends on the project you are working on and personal preference. Avoid leaving a needle in the fabric unless it is gold plated or it may cause marks. A beading needle (or fine 'sharp' needle), which is much thinner, will be needed to attach beads.
Scissors Use dressmaker's shears for cutting fabric and a small, sharp pair of pointed scissors for cutting embroidery threads.
Frames and hoops These are not essential but if you use one, choose one large enough to hold the complete design to avoid marking the fabric and flattening stitches.

Basic Techniques

The following pages describe how to prepare fabric for work, how to use the charts and how to work the stitches.

Preparing Fabric for Work

Press embroidery fabric before you begin stitching and trim the selvage or any rough edges. Work from the middle of the fabric and middle of the chart to ensure the design is centred on the fabric. Find the middle of the fabric by folding it in four and pressing lightly, then mark the folds with tailor's chalk or tacking (basting) stitches following a fabric thread. When working with linen sew a narrow hem around all raw edges to preserve them for finishing later.

Stitch Count and Design Size

Each project gives details of the stitch count and finished design size but if you wish to work the design on a different count fabric you will need to be able to calculate the finished size. Count the number of stitches in the design and divide this by the fabric count number, e.g., 140 stitches x 140 stitches ÷ by 14-count = a design size of 10 x 10in (25.4 x 25.4cm). Remember that working on evenweave usually means working over two threads not one, so divide the fabric count by two before you start.

Reading the Charts

The designs in this book are worked from colour charts, with symbols where necessary. Each square, both occupied and unoccupied, represents two threads of linen or one block of Aida. Each occupied square equals one stitch. Some designs use three-quarter cross stitches, shown as a triangle in a grid square. Some designs use French knots and beads and these are labelled in the key.

Starting and Finishing Stitching

Unless indicated otherwise, begin stitching in the middle of a design to ensure an adequate margin for making up. Start and finish stitching neatly, avoiding knots which create lumps.

Knotless loop start This neat start can be used with an even number of strands i.e., 2, 4 or 6. To stitch with two strands, begin with one strand about 80cm (30in). Double it and thread the needle with the two ends. Put the needle up through the fabric from the wrong side, where you intend to begin stitching, leaving the loop at the back. Form a half cross stitch, put the needle back through the fabric and through the waiting loop. The stitch is now anchored and you can begin.

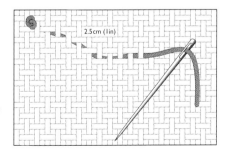

Away waste knot start Start this way if using an odd number of strands or when tweeding threads. Thread your needle with the number of strands required and knot the end. Insert the needle into the right side of the fabric about 2.5cm (1in) away from where you wish to begin stitching. Stitch towards the knot and cut it off when the threads are anchored. Alternatively, snip off the knot, thread the needle and work under a few stitches to anchor.

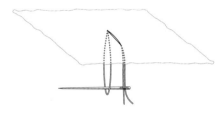

Finishing stitching At the back of the work, pass the needle and thread under several stitches of the same or similar colour and then snip off the loose end close to the stitching. You can begin a new colour in a similar way.

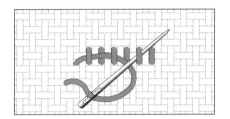

Working the Stitches

The projects in this book use basic stitches that are very easy to work: simply follow the instructions and diagrams below and overleaf.

Backstitch

Backstitch is used for outlining a design or part of a design, to add detail or emphasis, or for lettering. It is added after the cross stitch has been completed so the backstitch line isn't broken by cross stitches. It is shown on charts by a solid coloured line.

Follow the numbered sequence in the diagram, working the stitches over one block of Aida or over two threads of evenweave, unless stated otherwise on the chart.

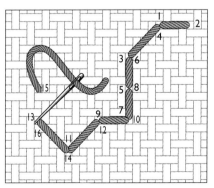

Cross Stitch

This is the most commonly used stitch in this book and can be worked singly or in two journeys. For neat stitching keep the top stitch facing the same direction. Half cross stitch is simply a single diagonal line.

Cross stitch on Aida Cross stitch on Aida fabric is normally worked over one block of the fabric.

To work a complete cross stitch, follow the numbered sequence in the diagram below: bring the needle up through the fabric at 1, cross one block of the fabric and insert the needle at 2. Push the needle through and bring it up at 3, ready to complete the stitch at 4. To work the adjacent stitch, bring the needle up at the bottom right-hand corner of the first stitch.

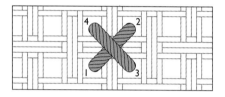

To work cross stitches in two journeys, work the first leg of the cross stitch as above but instead of completing the stitch, work the adjacent half stitch and continue on to the end of the row. Complete all the crosses by working the other diagonals on the return journey.

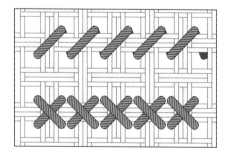

Cross stitch on evenweave Cross stitch on evenweave is usually worked over two threads of the fabric in each direction to even out any oddities in the thickness of the fibres. Bring the needle up to the left of a vertical thread to make it easier to spot counting mistakes. Work your cross stitch in two directions, in a sewing movement, half cross stitch in one direction and then

work back and cover the original stitches with the second row. This forms neat, single vertical lines on the back and gives somewhere to finish off raw ends.

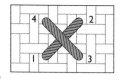

Three-quarter Cross Stitch

Three-quarter cross stitch is a fractional stitch which produces the illusion of curves. The stitch can be formed on Aida and evenweave but is more successful on evenweave. It is shown on charts as a triangle (half square).

Work the first half of a cross stitch as usual. Work the second 'quarter' stitch over the top and down into the central hole to anchor the first half of the stitch. If using Aida, you will need to push the needle through the centre of a block of the fabric. Where two three-quarter stitches lie back-to-back in the space of one full cross stitch, work both of the respective 'quarter' stitches into the central hole.

French Knot

French knots are small but important stitches that are used to add detail to a design. They are shown on charts as coloured circles.

Bring the needle through to the front of the fabric and wind the thread around the needle twice, or as directed in the project instructions. Begin to 'post' the needle partly through to the back, one thread or part of an Aida block away from the entry point. (This will stop the stitch being pulled to the wrong side.) Gently pull the thread you have wound

so that it sits snugly at the point where the needle enters the fabric. Pull the needle through to the back and you should have a perfect knot in position. For bigger French knots, it is best to add more strands of thread to the needle rather than winding more times.

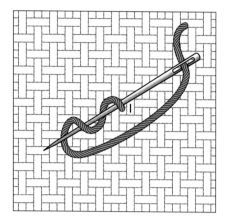

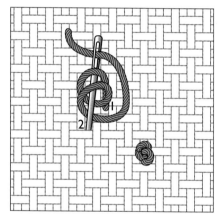

Long Stitch

Long straight stitches are used in some of the designs and they can be worked on any fabric. Simply bring the needle and thread up where the stitch is to start, at 1, and down where the chart indicates it should finish, at 2.

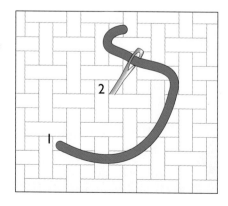

Working With Beads and Charms

Some of the designs in the book use beads and charms to bring an extra sparkle and dimension. Beads are shown on the charts as a large coloured circle with a dot, with details of the bead type in the key. You might find using a frame or hoop helpful to keep the fabric taut. Attach beads and charms using a beading needle or very fine 'sharp' needle, thread which matches the bead colour and a half or full cross stitch.

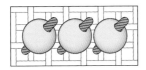

Making Up

The designs have been made up into many different items, as described in the project instructions. There are also plenty of suggestions throughout for other ways to display your work.

Making your own cards and mounting work in cards – see pages 32 and 33.

Making up a framed picture – see page 46.

Making up a wall hanging or banner – see page 9.

Making up a bag – see pages 74 and 88.

Making up a pincushion – see page 76.

Perfect Stitching

Organize your threads before you start a project as this will help to avoid confusion later. Put threads on an organizer (available from craft shops) and always include the manufacturer's name and the shade number.

★

Separate the strands on a skein of stranded cotton (floss) before taking the number you need, realigning them and threading your needle.

★

When stitching with metallic threads, work with shorter lengths, about 30cm (12in) to avoid tangling and excessive wear on the thread.

★

If using a frame, try to avoid a hoop as it will stretch the fabric and leave a mark that may be difficult to remove.

★

Plan your route carefully around the chart, counting over short distances where possible to avoid mistakes.

★

Work your cross stitch in two directions in a sewing movement – half cross stitch in one direction and then cover those original stitches with the second row. This forms vertical lines on the back and gives somewhere to finish off raw ends tidily. For neat work the top stitches should all face the same direction.

★

If adding a backstitch outline, always add it after the cross stitch has been completed to prevent the solid line being broken.

DMC/Anchor Thread Conversion

The designs in this book use DMC stranded cottons (floss). This DMC/Anchor thread conversion chart is only a guide, as exact colour comparisons cannot always be made. An asterisk * indicates an Anchor shade that has been used more than once so take care to avoid duplication in a design. If you wish to use Madeira threads, telephone for a conversion chart on 01845 524880 or e-mail: arts@madeira.co.uk

DMC	Anchor	DMC	Anchor	DMC	Anchor	DMC	Anchor	DMC	Anchor	DMC	Anchor	DMC	Anchor	DMC	Anchor
B 5200	1	355	1014	604	55	781	308*	912	209	3023	899	3765	170	3846	1090
White	2	356	1013*	605	1094	782	308*	913	204	3024	388*	3766	167	3847	1076*
Ecru	387*	367	216	606	334	783	307	915	1029	3031	905*	3768	779	3848	1074*
150	59	368	214	608	330*	791	178	917	89	3032	898*	3770	1009	3849	1070*
151	73	369	1043	610	889	792	941	918	341	3033	387*	3772	1007	3850	188*
152	969	370	888*	611	898*	793	176*	919	340	3041	871	3773	1008	3851	186*
153	95*	371	887*	612	832	794	175	920	1004	3042	870	3774	778	3852	306*
154	873	372	887*	613	831	796	133	921	1003*	3045	888*	3776	1048*	3853	1003*
155	1030*	400	351	632	936	797	132	922	1003*	3046	887*	3777	1015	3854	313
156	118*	402	1047*	640	393	798	146	924	851	3047	887	3778	1013*	3855	311*
157	120*	407	914	642	392	799	145	926	850	3051	845*	3779	868	3856	347
158	178	413	236*	644	391	800	144	927	849	3052	844	3781	1050	3857	936*
159	120*	414	235*	645	273	801	359	928	274	3053	843	3782	388*	3858	1007
160	175*	415	398	646	8581*	806	169	930	1035	3064	883	3787	904*	3859	914*
161	176	420	374	647	1040	807	168	931	1034	3072	397	3790	904*	3860	379*
162	159*	422	372	648	900	809	130	932	1033	3078	292	3799	236*	3861	378
163	877	433	358	666	46	813	161*	934	852*	3325	129	3801	1098	3862	358*
164	240*	434	310	676	891	814	45	935	861	3326	36	3802	1019*	3863	379*
165	278*	435	365	677	361*	815	44	936	846	3328	1024	3803	69	3864	376
166	280*	436	363	680	901*	816	43	937	268*	3340	329	3804	63*	3865	2*
167	375*	437	362	699	923*	817	13*	938	381	3341	328	3805	62*	3866	926*
168	274*	444	291	700	228	818	23*	939	152*	3345	268*	3806	62*	48	1207
169	849*	445	288	701	227	819	271	943	189	3346	267*	3807	122	51	1220*
208	110	451	233	702	226	820	134	945	881	3347	266*	3808	1068	52	1209*
209	109	452	232	703	238	822	390	946	332	3348	264	3809	1066*	57	1203*
210	108	453	231	704	256*	823	152*	947	330*	3350	77	3810	1066*	61	1218*
211	342	469	267*	712	926	824	164	948	1011	3354	74	3811	1060	62	1202*
221	897*	470	266*	718	88	825	162*	950	4146	3362	263	3812	188	67	1212
223	895	471	265	720	326	826	161*	951	1010	3363	262	3813	875*	69	1218*
224	895	472	253	721	324	827	160	954	203*	3364	261	3814	1074	75	1206*
225	1026	498	1005	722	323*	828	9159	955	203*	3371	382	3815	877*	90	1217*
300	352	500	683	725	305*	829	906	956	40*	3607	87	3816	876*	91	1211
301	1049*	501	878	726	295*	830	277*	957	50	3608	86	3817	875*	92	1215*
304	19	502	877*	727	293	831	277*	958	187	3609	85	3818	923*	93	1210*
307	289	503	876*	729	890	832	907*	959	186	3685	1028	3819	278	94	1216
309	42	504	206*	730	845*	833	874*	961	76*	3687	68	3820	306	95	1209*
310	403	517	162*	731	281*	834	874*	962	75*	3688	75*	3821	305*	99	1204
311	148	518	1039	732	281*	838	1088	963	23*	3689	49	3822	295*	101	1213*
312	979	519	1038	733	280	839	1086	964	185	3705	35*	3823	386	102	1209*
315	1019*	520	862*	734	279	840	1084	966	240	3706	33*	3824	8*	103	1210*
316	1017	522	860	738	361*	841	1082	970	925	3708	31	3825	323*	104	1217*
317	400	523	859	739	366	842	1080	971	316*	3712	1023	3826	1049*	105	1218*
318	235*	524	858	740	316*	844	1041	972	298	3713	1020	3827	311	106	1203*
319	1044*	535	401	741	304	869	375	973	290	3716	25	3828	373	107	1203*
320	215	543	933	742	303	890	218	975	357	3721	896	3829	901*	108	1220*
321	47	550	101*	743	302	891	35*	976	1001	3722	1027	3830	5975	111	1218*
322	978	552	99	744	301	892	33*	977	1002	3726	1018	3831	29	112	1201*
326	59*	553	98	745	300	893	27	986	246	3727	1016	3832	28	113	1210*
327	101*	554	95	746	275	894	26	987	244	3731	76*	3833	31*	114	1213*
333	119	561	212	747	158	895	1044*	988	243	3733	75*	3834	100*	115	1206*
334	977	562	210	754	1012	898	380	989	242	3740	872	3835	98*	121	1210*
335	40*	563	208	758	9575	899	38	991	1076	3743	869	3836	90	122	1215*
336	150	564	206*	760	1022	900	333	992	1072	3746	1030	3837	100*	124	1210*
340	118	580	924	761	1021	902	897*	993	1070	3747	120	3838	177	125	1213*
341	117*	581	281*	762	234	904	258	995	410	3750	1036	3839	176*	126	1209*
347	1025	597	1064	772	259*	905	257	996	433	3752	1032	3840	120*		
349	13*	598	1062	775	128	906	256*	3011	856	3753	1031	3841	159*		
350	11	600	59*	776	24	907	255	3012	855	3755	140	3842	164*		
351	10	601	63*	778	968	909	923*	3013	853	3756	1037	3843	1089*		
352	9	602	57	779	380*	910	230	3021	905*	3760	162*	3844	410*		
353	8*	603	62*	780	309	911	205	3022	8581*	3761	928	3845	1089*		

Suppliers

UK

The American Way
30 Edgbaston Road, Smethwick,
West Midlands B66 4LQ
tel: 0121 601 5454
*For Mill Hill buttons, charms, wire
hangers and many other supplies*

Coats Crafts UK
PO Box 22, Lingfield Estate,
McMullen Road, Darlington,
County Durham DL1 1YQ
tel: 01325 365457 (for a list of stockists)
*For Anchor stranded cotton (floss) and
other embroidery supplies (Coats also
supply some Charles Craft products)*

Craft Creations Ltd.
1C Ingersoll House, Delamare Road,
Cheshunt, Herts EN8 9HD
tel: 01992 781900
website: www.craftcreations.com
*For greetings card blanks and card-
making accessories*

From Debbie Cripps
31 Lower Whitelands,
Radstock, Bath BA3 3JW
website: www.debbiecripps.co.uk
For buttons and charms

Dee Fine Arts
182 Telegraph Road,
Heswall, Wirral CH60 0AJ
tel: 0151 342 6657
For expert embroidery framing

DMC Creative World
Pullman Road, Wigston,
Leicestershire LE18 2DY
tel: 0116 281 1040
website: www.dmc/cw.com
*For a huge range of threads, fabrics
and needlework supplies*

Framecraft Miniatures Ltd.
372–376 Summer Lane, Hockley,
Birmingham B19 3QA
tel: 0121 212 0551
website: www.framecraft.com
*For Mill Hill buttons, charms, wooden
and ceramic trinket pots, notebook
covers and many other pre-finished
items with cross stitch inserts*

Gregory Knopp
PO Box 158,
Gillingham, Kent ME7 3HF
tel: 01634 375706
website: www.gregory-knopp.co.uk
For folk-art buttons

USA

Charles Craft Inc.
PO Box 1049,
Laurenburg, NC 28353
tel: 910 844 3521
email: ccraft@carolina.net
website: www.charlescraft.com
*Cross stitch fabrics and many useful
pre-finished items*

Design Works Crafts Inc.
170 Wilbur Place,
Bohemia, New York 11716
tel: 631 244 5749
email:
customerservice@designworkscrafts.com
*For cross stitch kits featuring Joan Elliott
designs and for card mounts*

Gay Bowles Sales Inc.
PO Box 1060,
Janesville, WI 53547
tel: 608 754 9466
email: millhill@inwave.com
website: www.millhill.com
*For Mill Hill beads and a US source for
Framecraft products*

Kreinik Manufacturing Company Inc.
3106 Timanus Lane, Suite 101,
Baltimore, MD 21244
tel: 1800 537 2166
email: kreinik@kreinik.com
website: www.kreinik.com
For a wide range of metallic threads

The WARM Company
954 East Union Street,
Seattle, WA 98122
tel: 1 800 234 WARM
website: www.warmcompany.com
UK Distributor: W. Williams & Sons Ltd
Regent House, 1 Thane Villas,
London N7 7PH
tel: 0207 263 7311
www.wwilliams.co.uk
*For polyester filling, cotton wadding
(batting) and Steam-a-Seam fusible web*

Zweigart/Joan Toggit Ltd.
262 Old Brunswick Road, Suite E,
Piscataway, NJ 08854-3756
tel: 732 562 8888
email: info@zweigart.com
website: www.zweigart.com
*For a large selection of cross stitch
fabrics and pre-finished table linens*

Our Angelic Designers

Sue Cook

Sue's wonderful designs appear regularly in needlecraft magazines, including *Cross Stitcher*, *Cross Stitch Collection* and *World of Cross Stitching*. Her three most recent books, *Cross Stitch Inspirations*, *Sue Cook's Wonderful Cross Stitch Collection* and *Sue Cook's Bumper Cross Stitch Collection* were all published by David & Charles. Sue lives with her husband, Ade, in Newport, South Wales.

Joan Elliott

Joan's creations have been enchanting cross stitch enthusiasts the world over for years, and she is a leading artist for Design Works Crafts Inc. Her debut book for David & Charles, *A Cross Stitcher's Oriental Odyssey* was followed by *Cross Stitch Teddies* and her third book, *Cross Stitch Sentiments & Sayings* is publishing in May 2004. Joan divides her time between New York and Vermont.

Claire Crompton

Claire studied knitwear design at college, before joining the design team at DMC, and finally going freelance. Claire's work has appeared in several magazines, including *Cross Stitch Magic*. Her designs also feature in *Cross Stitch Greetings Cards* and *Cross Stitch Alphabets*, as well as in her new book *Cross Stitch Card Collection*, all published by David & Charles. Claire lives in the Tamar Valley, Cornwall.

Helen Philipps

Helen's needlepoint and cross stitch designs feature regularly in stitching magazines. An interest in samplers and gardening led to the publication of two books for David & Charles, *The New Cross Stitch Sampler Book* and *Helen Philipps' Cross Stitch Garden Notebook*, and she is now working on a new book, *Cross Stitch Samplers & Cards*. Helen runs Merry Heart Designs, and lives in the Wirral.

Maria Diaz

Maria studied fine art and painting at university. She then became DMC's first in-house designer, before working as a specialist consultant on a craft publication. Her work now appears regularly in craft magazines. Maria has contributed to three previous David & Charles titles: *Cross Stitch Alphabets*, *Cross Stitch Greetings Cards* and *Cross Stitch Myth & Magic*. Maria lives in Staffordshire.

Lesley Teare

Lesley trained as a textile designer, with a degree in printed and woven textiles. For some years she has been one of DMC's leading designers and her designs have also featured in many of the popular cross stitch magazines. Lesley has contributed to two other books for David & Charles, *Cross Stitch Greetings Cards* and *Cross Stitch Alphabets*. Lesley lives in Hitcham, Suffolk.

Acknowledgments

The publishers would like to thank the following designers for their beautiful contributions: Sue Cook, Claire Crompton, Maria Diaz, Joan Elliott, Helen Philipps and Lesley Teare.

Additional thanks to Kim Sayer and Lucy Mason for the photography and to Lin Clements for her continuous attention to detail in charting and editing.

Index

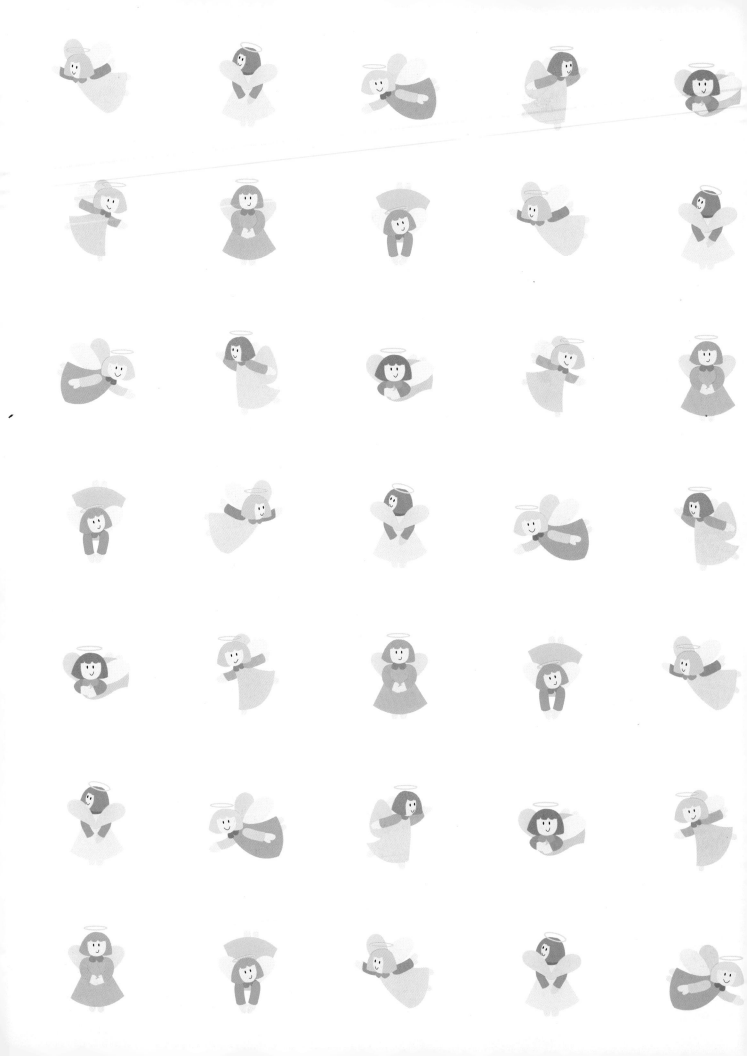